What Would Judy Say?

A Grown-Up Guide

To

Living Together

(With Benefits)

Judge Judy Sheindlin

What Would Judy Say?

Judge Judy Sheindlin
Copyright © 2013 Judy Sheindlin
Printed in the United States of America

* * * * *

Credits

Cover photo by Robert Piazza Photographer, LLC
www.robertpiazza.com

Cover design by Laura Duffy

Illustrations by Wally Littman

Formatting by Debora Lewis
arenapublishing.org

* * * * *

To the thousands of people who shared
their stories on my Web site,
www.whatwouldjudysay.com.
It is my hope that their experiences will
help negotiate life's journey for many
others.

Table of Contents

Introduction: Warriors and Maidens 1

Chapter 1: The Quest to Nest 7

Chapter 2: Frogs Don't Become Princes 17

Chapter 3: Get Off the Pot 25

Chapter 4: Common Sense Is Not Common 39

Chapter 5: Kids in the Picture 55

Chapter 6: What's Mine Is (NOT) Yours 65

Chapter 7: There's No Relationship Fairy 79

Chapter 8: The EX Factor 87

Chapter 9: The Art of Cohabiting 93

Chapter 10: There Ought to Be a Law 105

Conclusion: Imperfect Unions 107

Introduction: Warriors and Maidens

You learn a lot living with someone. Several weeks before my stepdaughter Nicole was going to get married, she and her intended, Dan, were cleaning their tiny studio apartment. It was his turn to do the bathroom, and she was going to do the kitchen. She called to tell me what happened next, because it was so alarming to her. "He came into the kitchen and took the sponge near the sink," she said with an awestruck tone. "Then he went into the bathroom and cleaned the toilet. Then he came back into the kitchen, rinsed the sponge and put it back next to the sink. I am so appalled by his thought process, I don't know what to do."

So I told her, "Sweetheart, men are warriors, and warriors don't clean up after themselves. If forced to do so, they will exhibit remarkable ineptitude until you finally beg them to let you take care of it yourself. This is one of the adult lessons you learn when you live with a man." (Her father is a prime example of that. If Jerry is confronted with a task that is unpleasant for him—something he doesn't want to incorporate into his chore life—he will just try to do it once badly.)

I think Nicole got my point, because fifteen years later she and Dan have a lovely marriage and wonderful kids. They get along beautifully, although he occasionally reminds Nicole of his warrior status. When Dan saw a small leak in the basement, he stuck a Dixie cup under it to catch the water and promptly forgot about it. By the time Nicole noticed, it was Niagara Falls. *Warrior*.

"WHEN YOU'RE FINISHED CONQUERING MARS, PLEASE, PLEASE GET ME A NEW SHOVEL."

Everybody has idiosyncratic behavior. The goal is to achieve a balance between what you're willing to put up with and whether it's worth the return you get. It's all about compromise, knowing that at the end of the day your ultimate goal is to create a strong, happy, long-term relationship.

Women are the nesters, the gatherers and the peacemakers. Warriors keep us safe from Genghis Khan and the hordes, and while not protecting the farm must be kept calm and productive. When I need to have a conversation with Jerry that I know is going to be unpleasant, I do it when we're in the car. That's because when warriors are forced to look an adversary in the eye, they get combative. Jerry is less likely to be upset if he can't see the whites of my eyes.

This is a grown-up guide to living together, which means we'll be facing reality about the warriors and their maidens, who choose to embark upon a grand adventure of living together with benefits. It's a whole new world, but the basic rules are as old as time.

When I was young, you either left your parents' house in a white dress or a pine box. The norms have changed. Living together without benefit of marriage is now common. At the last census, 45 percent of all households were unmarried couples. I don't have a problem with people living together before marriage—there's something to be said for testing the waters—but you've got to be smart. To quote a favorite African proverb, "Only a fool tests the depth of the water by jumping in with both feet."

My TV courtroom is filled with disillusioned and financially devastated former live-ins. They are stunned to learn that there is no law to protect them, and too often the stars in their eyes prevented them from seeing clearly that they should have established some rules. They cry, "It's not fair!" when their love and live-in arrangements dissolve, leaving them with a pile of bills, car payments for vehicles they no longer possess, and bare cupboards. They resent being in a bind from broken promises that they never bothered to memorialize in writing because they were "in love." But as Mae West (I didn't personally know her) once said, "An ounce of performance is worth pounds of promises." As long as you are living together and testing the waters, there should be rules. There are divorce laws, but none for just cohabiting. There is no Court of People Living Together.

Recently, one of my kids said to me, "Until you live with somebody, you're really just meeting the *representative* of the person." I thought it was a smart comment—and it's one reason why living together for a brief time is not such a bad idea. It gives you a chance to meet the real human being behind the representative and decide whether or not he or she is the one you want to spend your life with. This book is about that process.

Between my time in a courtroom, my time as a TV judge dealing with relationship problems, and my life as a woman who has been married, divorced, remarried, and had children and stepchildren and exes, I feel as if I've seen it all. What you'll read in this book is not gospel, but my seasoned opinion. I've got some strong ideas about people living together before marriage.

This book is the first in a series of relationship books, based on my Web site, *What Would Judy Say?* When I put the topic of "roommates with benefits" to readers on my Web site, the floodgates opened and the pent-up waters of wisdom, outrage, and regret came pouring through. There were lots of hard-luck stories, but also some great wisdom shared by those who have been there, done that, and have no intention of ever doing it again. The mission statement of the Web site is simple: if people share their stories, perhaps they will help a friend or a stranger from making the same mistake—or at least get them to think about it before making the same mistake. I respect and enjoy the wit and wisdom of my viewers and readers. Often, they tell me they've learned invaluable lessons from watching *Judge Judy*. I learn from them as well.

This is an adult handbook for anyone considering making the leap to a live-in arrangement before marriage. I'll share the cautionary tales of roommates with benefits, and some advice. Sometimes, for those blinded by love or lust, there are no benefits—just *tsuris*, meaning aggravation. My hope is that you can save yourself some of that. Read on.

Chapter 1: The Quest to Nest

Jerry and I had been together for a year and a half. I wanted a commitment. He wanted the whole package without the legality. He would have been happy living together, and even uttered those immortal words about a marriage license: "It's just a piece of paper." (I've rarely heard this description from a woman, but it's a favorite with men.) "Why does the state have to get involved?" he asked plaintively. "We're already in a committed relationship."

But I was looking at things another way. I was thirty-two years old—at my prime. I looked terrific, I had a career, and I already had a couple of kids. Now I wanted a nest, and I was faced with the fact that he did not. I didn't have great leverage. Jerry wasn't afraid of me. However, my father was another story, so I wisely suggested, "Go ask my father. If he agrees, we'll live together." Without missing a beat, Jerry replied, "Okay, we'll get married."

I remember sitting in a bagel shop on Third Avenue in Manhattan while we were having this discussion. I took out my little Filofax, and said to him, "Pick a date."

Well, Jerry has a wonderful sense of humor, and he thought that was funny. He laughed. "Okay, how about Flag Day?"

"Good." I wrote it in my book. Then I stood up from the table. "I'll be right back." I went to the pay phone on the corner—they didn't have cell phones in those days—and I called my mother. "We're getting married on Flag Day," I told her. "Go find a place." Jerry hardly knew what hit him.

If you spoke with Jerry today, he would probably say that it was the best decision he *almost* made in his life. I love being married to Jerry Sheindlin. But in the beginning, I had the urge to own the nest, and he just wanted to rent it.

That being said, I think there is merit to living together for a while. Today, if you want a nest—and let's face it, most women do—living together can rightly be viewed as the first step. All of our kids lived together with their partners for a while before they got married. I think it did provide at least a brief window into what they were getting themselves into and what their mates were getting themselves into. But if your ultimate goal is the nest, with a marriage license, you have to finalize it within a reasonable period. Otherwise, it's time to reevaluate your options.

Let me speak frankly. Time is an issue, because the sad reality is that women have a shorter blooming period than men. There are fertility issues. We look our physical best at a certain age. The Dolly Parton character in the movie *Steel Magnolias* noted, "Honey, time marches on and eventually you realize it's marchin' across your face," and that's true. When you are a forty five year-old woman who's never been married, the opportunity for you is different because an age-appropriate guy is thinking, "Younger is better." It's not pretty, but it's a reality.

So women who are looking forward to marriage and kids have to be careful that they don't get stuck wasting their time living with a guy who has a different agenda. If you feel a strong enough commitment that you're willing to live with someone, you should have a reasonable expectation that marriage will follow, if that's what you want.

We all know couples who are the almost-marrieds. They live together. They share friends. They go on vacation together. They attend functions together. They do charity work together. They're together in every way but being married. I don't know one of those couples where the gal doesn't want more than a promise ring. I even know a woman in a longtime living-together arrangement who casually refers to her mate as "my husband." She says it's easier, but nobody's fooled. The men in these relationships are likely to say, "I love you, honey, but I've been there, done that. We will be together as a couple but I don't want to marry again." And the women stay, even though it's not what they want. They don't look around for someone else who might be ready to get married. They love their partners and they trust them. They work at it like a marriage, but it's not a marriage. Meanwhile, the longer they stay, the more their chances of marching to the altar diminish. If the relationship fails, they're out of luck. Some people can look for a new chicken while they keep the old one in the pot. Most cannot.

Tiffany's rule

Tiffany was a young woman, but she balked at living with her mate until he signed on the dotted line.

"When my husband and I were just dating, he would have been more than happy to live with me. Because I wanted to get married eventually, I wasn't going to live with him (or any man, for that matter). Why would he want to marry me if he already had everything that would come with married life? (Why buy the cow when you can get the milk for free?) His brother has lived with the mother of his children for many years and still hasn't married her. He always says, 'What's the rush?'"

Judge Judy says: Famous last words: "We weren't ready to make that commitment." I can understand if a couple wasn't ready to make a permanent commitment and they had an accident and got pregnant. But *three* accidents? I see these couples in my courtroom. They tell me with straight faces, "We want to be *sure* before we get married and make that kind of commitment." Or worse, "We were saving up for the wedding."

Today, living together is common. Even so, you'd be surprised how many times young women quote the adage, "Why buy the cow when you can get the milk for free?" I can only surmise that there is an essential truth to that idea.

In Angela's case, he got more than milk.

Angela's hard fall

"Through a series of unfortunate events, I ended up living with my husband before we got married. It was the worst decision I had ever made. It was I who was the roommate. He had the benefits. From the start I paid almost 100 percent of expenses, performed 100 percent of the housework, and performed 75 percent of the yard work. I also cooked, washed, dried, folded, and ironed, not to mention held down a job where I worked ten hours per day. Needless to say, I was exhausted by the end of the week. He was supposed to start helping financially when he got out of credit-card debt from his past marriage and family, but that day never arrived.

'Romeo' slowly withdrew and then redirected his affections."

Judge Judy says: Angela's Romeo had a great deal going for him. It sort of reminds me of the trip Jerry and I took to Africa a few years ago. While on safari, we came across a pride of lions. The two females, who were mothering their cubs, had also just concluded a hunting mission and had brought back a large wildebeest. The male lion, who heretofore had been sitting under a tree in the shade, fanning himself with his tail, was presented with this prize. He proceeded to covet it and would not allow either the two females who had procured the meat or the cubs to partake until he had finished stuffing his face.

This whole scene was amusing to me, and I became curious about what exactly the function of the male lion was in the pride. Since he did not bear the children, care for them, or procure the food—what did he *do*? A little investigation suggested that the sole function of the male, after his procreative duties were completed, was to protect himself from other males who might want to send him packing.

It was also instructive for me to find out that the life span of the male lion is generally shorter than that of the female. Based on what we've heard for the past thirty-odd years, if you exercise and exert yourself, chances are you'll live longer. The fact that the male lion does nothing but screw and eat contributes to his shorter life span. It makes you wonder—how did *he* become the king of the jungle? Something's not right.

If you follow that thread to humans, you need only look at the state of Florida, where I live. There are many, many more widows than widowers. Oddly, the difference in life spans is about the same as that for lions. Maybe the women are doing what Angela did—*everything*.

Angela bought into this plan and ended up feeling used. She didn't understand how Romeo could dump her when she did so much for him. She thought she could make her man love her by being his everything. She was a whirlwind of caretaking, cooking, and cleaning—even landscaping. She made a big mistake, thinking it would make her loved and indispensable.

Here's a story about the reality I knew long before I was Judge Judy. My friend Elaine and I were walking with our two babies, and it was a beautiful day. She said, "I really have to get back because Brian is coming home soon and I haven't finished cleaning the bathroom." I just looked at her, dumbfounded, and said, "Elaine, no man ever rushed home to a clean toilet." The words were true then—and now.

Angela was working overtime, but her mate still withdrew his affection. If she had pampered herself and spent her time getting a bikini wax and a great pedicure, getting a facial once a week, having her hair blown out, maybe he would have noticed. Instead, she chose to become a martyr. She really thought if he saw how hard she was working, how neat she kept his closet, how beautifully she served his main course, how brilliantly the toilets sparkled, he'd be turned on. Men don't care about that stuff. They want something that smells good—and I'm not talking meat loaf.

Melanie's bad choices

Melanie abided by the rule, "If at first you don't succeed, try, try again." In her case, it was one big trial.

"I made the mistake of living with three boyfriends in my twenties. After the third cohabiting experience, I learned my lesson. First time, I was twenty-one, he was twenty-four. We had separate accounts and split all bills. It lasted eight months. Second time, we were both twenty-four, together one year, and moved to New York ten days after my graduation. It was hard to secure full-time work right away and this added stress to the relationship. We

lasted nine months in New York. We did not share a bank account. Third time, we lived together four years. He ended up being a drunk. We maintained our own accounts but had a joint one for bills. Luckily I trusted my intuition and decided to give myself six months to get everything in order before I broke up with him. This included closing the joint account so he couldn't drain it out of spite. I will never again live with someone unless I marry him! If I have to deal with a man every day in my space, it might as well be legal."

Judge Judy says: Hopefully the third time was the charm for Melanie. In general, if you can't decide within a year whether to get married, it's probably wrong. Don't marry just for the sake of making it legal. That's plain dumb. Marriage to a loser is a losing proposition.

Julie's lesson: Adults only

It's fair to say that living together successfully is reserved for grown-ups. Julie gained a kid and lost her son in the process.

"My son was twenty and in college. He met a girl who was eighteen and had just been asked to leave her mother and stepfather's home. They all didn't get along. Against my better judgment, I allowed her to move in and share a room with my son. What a nightmare. She was a slob who contributed nothing

but stress and hair in the sink. When they fought, which was often, there was no peace. But I was stuck and couldn't get rid of her without alienating my son. She finally convinced him that I was the troublemaker and he moved out, dropped out of school, got a dead-end job to support her, and I never see him. What an idiot."

Judge Judy says: Living together does not mean kids shacking up in Mommy's house. As a judge I have heard dozens of cases involving people taking other people's children into their homes to play house with their children. My best and only advice is do not do it. It's better to have an empty nest than a hornet's nest.

Chapter 2: Frogs Don't Become Princes

Being a nurturer need not equate with being a moron. A young woman in my courtroom who was robbed blind by her boyfriend explained her temporary insanity by saying, "He told me it was destiny for us to be together." The truth is not always what we want to hear. *Love* doesn't have to be blind, and *crazy* doesn't cut it with the bill collectors.

If I were asked to define "love crazy," I would say the following:

Love crazy is getting involved with a so-so guy or gal, and then creating a fantasy around them that is lacking in reality.

Love crazy is failing to notice the alcohol and drugs in the first couple months of a relationship.

Love crazy is thinking that he or she will become smarter or more responsible after you're together and have worked your magic.

Love crazy is swooning—and keep in mind that when you're swooning, you're not conscious. Do you get that? You are Not Awake.

Love crazy is being obsessed with beautiful eyes or a great body, but never noticing what's going on inside because you're too busy drooling over the package.

Love crazy is making excuses for outlandish flaws. You'll say things like:

* ❖ "He never had a job because of the bad economy."

* ❖ "She drinks too much—on the weekends (uh-huh, just the weekends)—because she needs to unwind."

* ❖ "His old girlfriends keep calling because they can't leave him alone. He's so understanding. He only talks to them to be polite."

* ❖ "The IRS is harassing her unfairly."

* ❖ "He only got fired because they were downsizing their top people."

Shall I continue? There's a Yiddish saying that when translated warns, "What you don't see with your eyes, don't invent with your mouth." I think it applies to fantasizing—to making up a pretty picture that isn't real.

When I was young, an unemployed man with a poor credit record, a pile of debt, no job, and a substance-abuse problem was considered a lousy catch. That's still true today, but many women think of themselves as reformers, not unlike the crusading Aimee Semple McPherson. They believe they can redo a fully grown man. When they delude themselves by trying to change character flaws in a partner, they're usually disappointed. Here, men are less guilty—they just move on.

When you're in love, you can be ruled not by your head, but by your hormones. The five senses are overwhelmed. You look into his deep blue eyes and feel lust and attachment, and you call it love. There's nothing new here. It's perfectly human. But humans also have brains, and even when the hormones are going wild, we're all capable of engaging those muscles in our heads that pull us back from the brink. My best advice can be summed up as follows: see things as they actually are, and then act accordingly. You can be in love without being a fool.

Lovesick Jane

Jane came close to being swept away, but fortunately she engaged her brain before her heart landed her in a pile of trouble.

"I went out with a guy for just over one year. At the time, I owned my own property and led a professional and independent life. Still do. He was approaching fifty. He swept me off my feet. However, when we discussed his creditworthiness, he was evasive. I decided to investigate. I could smell a rat. He had a county court judgment against him, he was up to his eyeballs in debt, he did not own his own home, and he was dodging the tax man. He was a bluffer. I had a lucky escape. Being associated with him in marriage would have meant I would have lost my home to him and his debts in one swoop of a pen. Be direct... quickly!"

Judge Judy says: Being swept away doesn't mean sweeping your brain clean of common sense. It's the old quack and duck. If it walks, looks, and quacks like a duck, it's usually a duck. People are marrying older and remarrying later, too. During that time they may have acquired houses, assets, a car, sometimes an inheritance, and all of those other things—savings, retirement funds, pensions, stocks and bonds. You really have to use your brain: "I love this guy, I love this woman, but I must use a little bit of a common sense in order to protect myself." A lifetime of responsible behavior can evaporate with one emotionally charged decision. Remember—ten times measure, one time cut.

Laura's folly

Unfortunately, even otherwise intelligent people fall prey to the crazies, as Laura's story demonstrates.

"As an educated woman, I can't figure out why I continue to believe that a duck will someday become a swan. No matter what I do, no amount of love, patience, support, or tears is going to change that. When I think of all the time, money, and heart I have wasted on ducks, it makes me so angry and sad. Ducks are cute and often fun to be around, but at the end of the day, they are no substitute for a swan. I can't help but wonder whether I would have made better choices if I had a mom like you. Can't change that duck either! So all I can do now is try not to make the same mistakes again."

Judge Judy says: The opposite of a duck is not a swan, although swans mate for life, which is a point in their favor. What I would say to Laura is that she is not helpless against mysterious forces. She is intelligent. She can make a reasonable choice without the drama.

Sharin's flawed prince

Sharin thought she'd found her prince. But she learned the hard way that he was a frog. Once a frog...

"It started as a love story. He was my prince. He protected me and I thought he shared my values. Then a year later, he became a shadow of something else. He was supposed to love me, but he had another woman, or shall I say several women. He had an addiction to drugs and a whole other life that I knew nothing about. I stayed with this man, this devil in sheep's clothing, for several years. I was scared to leave the only love I knew. Finally, I did leave this love. It was too painful, too hurtful. I had to let go."

Judge Judy says: This guy was never a prince. He never protected Sharin or cared a whit about her values. When I hear stories like this, I find myself getting curious. What did she see that enraptured her so thoroughly? You can't just blame hormones. She felt this man was "supposed" to love her. Why? Because they were breathing the same air? Because he was eating her food? Because he said he loved her—against all evidence? She probably saw signs of the truth early on and just decided to ignore them. Maybe she was lonely; maybe she thought she could change him. Remember what I said earlier: don't invent with your mouth what you don't see with your eyes.

Trust me. With few exceptions, adults don't change. A dishonest person doesn't become honest. A lazy, shiftless, spoiled, surly person won't magically morph into a diligent, responsible, delightful, selfless partner. Don't try to teach a pig to sing. It doesn't work, and it irritates the pig.

Thomas's blind love

In Thomas's case, the blindness came complete with a signed contract.

"I never really knew what was meant by the expression 'love is blind' until it applied to me. After living together for a few years, my partner and I decided to purchase our apartment. His mother, a woman of means, offered to lend us the money and we would pay her back on a monthly basis. Of course, we used her lawyer and I signed on the dotted line. Here's where I could have used a good pair of glasses. A few years later, my partner and I broke up. This time I got my own lawyer. To my surprise, I discovered he had never paid his share of the monthly payments. Therefore, not only was I to pay my remaining share of the loan to his mother, but his share as well! It was clearly stated in the documents I had signed, but never read—if one person defaults on

the payments, the other is responsible. A lesson well learned."

Judge Judy says: In any relationship—domestic, social, love affair, business, marital, maternal, paternal, friend—wipe the stardust out of your eyes before signing anything. Get somebody to take a second look. People get trapped all the time by the terms of agreements they didn't fully read and understand before signing. Having said that, this situation doesn't smell right. First, the lender is the partner's mother. Second, they used the mother's lawyer. Third, the loan was apparently in arrears without Thomas's knowledge. But whatever happened, the point is people have to wake up and take responsibility for their finances. Never just assume it's being handled. Look at the bank statements and the loan statements every month. That's not so hard, is it?

If I had a dollar for every time I heard, "But I trusted him," or "I trusted her," we could put a serious dent in the national debt. It's a delicious feeling to be crazy in love. I've been lucky to have that feeling for about forty years. It doesn't, however, mean blind, deaf, and without common sense. So use your noodles, folks. Enjoy the love, but stay grounded.

Chapter 3: Get Off the Pot

Living together is like taking a test-drive. If you're thinking about buying a car, the dealer may let you take it out for an afternoon. You'd get laughed out of the dealership if you said, "I'd like to test-drive this car for a year." The point is that the test-drive has a set parameter. If you don't bring the car back, the marshal will show up at your door. So in between the dating and the engagement, you have a test-drive called living together. Let us be clear that the test-drive is also a commitment. It's more than just sleeping and eating together.

People love the trappings! You start to use the word *we*: "We're planning a cruise... we're going to the country..." It feels nice. But there's more to commitment than a warm and fuzzy feeling you get when you use the word *we*.

In my courtroom I see that many people are confused about the idea of commitment. They just don't get what's expected of them. I think part of the reason—and forgive me for sidetracking into a little rant here—is that we live in a celebrity-crazed culture, and for better or worse, celebrities too often set the bar for common behavior. People look at celebrities and see their revolving-door relationships. They see them living together permanently, or their children being flower girls at their weddings. They see them "getting engaged" and staying that way for ten years, as if being engaged is a higher level of commitment. People think, "If Brad and Angelina can have a wonderful, free life with their six little kids, why can't I?" I would say to them, quite directly, "You are not Brad and Angelina."

When someone tells me they decided to buy a house, purchase a time-share, have a kid, get a pet, and share a bank account but they're not getting married because they're not ready to make that kind of commitment, I think maybe they should be committed—or at least have their head examined. Wake up: if you're sharing a domicile, a car, kids, and a pet, you *are* committed—only your commitment has a high level of risk. What you don't have is that piece of paper that protects you if things don't work out. Your problems are the lowest priority in the court system. They'll keep me in business until I'm one hundred!

Karen's blind commitment

In Karen's case, her guy told her he didn't have the time or impetus to be committed. He said it straight out. So what did she do? She convinced him that they should buy a condo together.

"After one year of dating, he told me he couldn't be my boyfriend as he didn't have the time to be attentive as a boyfriend should be. I said okay, and opened the door for him to leave. Three months later

we got back together and six months later we bought a condo together (my idea). From the day we met, I told him I would never, ever get rid of my cats just to have a man in my life. Six months after we signed a mortgage together, he told me, 'Sorry, I tried, I can't live with cats.' Of course I chose my cats. Eight months after living in the basement of my home, I moved out, and he stopped paying the mortgage and forced the condo into foreclosure. He continued to live there for almost a year RENT FREE! He made good money at his job while I worked three jobs, including my own home-based business. He never did one bit of basic housecleaning. My credit is even worse because of him."

Judge Judy says: Karen admits that it was her idea to buy a shared condo *after* he told her he didn't have time to be an attentive boyfriend. Not to mention his problem with the cats. I'll probably get in trouble for saying this, but I found it odd that Karen chose her cats over the person that she supposedly loved. We all love our animals, but if you want a committed relationship and your loved one is allergic, do you choose the cats?

Karen and her live-in boyfriend were spinning in separate orbits. They weren't communicating about their true feelings. They weren't communicating about the cats. Previous generations didn't communicate much. My grandparents only had two modes—silence and yelling. To the credit of most young couples today, they *do* communicate more. They look at a conflict and acknowledge that it's hard. They sit down and discuss it. They go to counseling if they can't work it out. It's not considered a failure to go to counseling—and I think that's terrific. Karen and her boyfriend let their true feelings fester until they became explosive.

Lack of communication is also the reason you have situations like Chloe's, where the supposed love of her life said he wasn't ready for commitment, but when they broke up, he married someone else right away. He wasn't ready for commitment with *Chloe*. That was the problem.

Chloe's commitment-phobic boyfriend

"After twenty-one years of marriage, my relationship fell apart when we had finished raising kids and a barrage of real-life issues hit. Several years later, I met a wonderful age-appropriate man. He was the best love of my life. He was reluctant to marry again, as he hadn't been divorced very long. I wanted commitment, especially since he was living in my home. We broke up our separate households and moved in together. My wise friend reminded me I was giving the milk for free and he would never marry me. After four years, I got a golf club for my birthday versus an engagement ring. In other words, no proposal but I got the titanium bubble shaft. He told me he wasn't ready. I told him I had choices too, and we partially parted ways for a few weeks. I was hoping he would miss me—wrong! I clearly told him I wanted him in my life. He responded that he had

found someone else and actually married her ninety days later."

Judge Judy says: If you want a marriage and it's not happening, show him the door. I spoke earlier about how Jerry and I came to the point of marriage mostly because I wanted the nest. But here's a detail. When Jerry and I started to get serious, he had a bit of unfinished business. Although he'd been legally separated from his wife for four years, they were still legally married. Jerry had kind of a sweet arrangement. He lived in the family house with the kids on the weekends, and this worked great for years. I wasn't buying this blissful scenario. I said, "It's over. Put a period on it. Life's a journey, but it's not an everlasting journey." But Jerry was concerned. "My kids don't want their parents to be divorced," he said.

It was the word *divorce* that bothered everybody. They had all settled into a very comfortable arrangement, and I was being incorporated into it. Everyone except me was happy with business as usual.

I know what Jerry was thinking: "I like my old house. I'm the one who built the shelves and finished the basement. It's still mine. I can have this lovely girlfriend too, and her car is nicer than mine."

But I had enough self-esteem to know I wasn't willing to settle for half-assed commitment. I wanted the wedding. On the anniversary of our meeting I gave him a special gift—luggage.

Jerry got his divorce and we were married. But get real, folks. Sometimes it's not that he's not the marrying kind. It's just that he's not marrying *you*. Maybe you're living a lie. I have seen this same scenario a number of times, not just in court, but in life. People spend five years, eight years, ten years waiting for a divorce to become final. And finally he (or she) announces that he has to vacate the apartment. "I'm getting married… to Shirley."

If you're in one of those eternal "almost married" situations, you have to be prepared to issue an ultimatum—and then stick to it. Never make an idle promise or a threat.

Dale gave her mate an ultimatum—and it worked!

Dale's ultimatum:

"My first marriage lasted all of three years. I swore I wouldn't marry again, but sixteen years later, I met my best friend and lover. We lived separately but had pajama parties every night. After four years we decided to move in together. We started to build a life together and when we saw a lawyer about making wills, we were advised that marriage was the best way to go, because of legal battles with our exes that could occur if one of us were to become ill or die. I gave him an ultimatum and he was down on his knee the next day with a ring and a proposal of marriage. Turns out, we really like being married. We like calling each other wife and husband. We like the

security we feel. It's been twenty years—who would have thought?"

Judge Judy says: There's nothing wrong with a well-applied nudge. It worked for Dale because her mate knew she wasn't bluffing, and he basically wanted the same thing she did.

Becky's heavy load

Becky saw the warning signs early and took action.

"I made the beginner's mistake of living with a guy without the commitment of marriage. After just a few short months, he wasn't as forthcoming with half of the rent as I was. I was carrying the load for both of us. It was when I noticed the new clothes in his closet that I had enough of his selfish ways. I kicked him out and have been happy ever since. I had thought about trying to go to court and getting back what I felt I was owed, but after watching many episodes of Judge Judy, *I realized that I also needed to learn this life lesson. I guarantee it never happened again."*

Judge Judy says: Hold on to that thought. It's smart to put a period on it and get moving as quickly as you can. My best advice is, don't make excuses. Don't repaint the picture. Take off the love-crazy blinders. Stay out of court if you can. You very rarely end up with a satisfying result, and nobody comes away happy.

Let's acknowledge that a lot of litigious behavior is actually about revenge. Some of it, however, is about keeping the other person in your life. You know the story. You buy a puppy together, and it's all wonderful. Then you break up, and you arrange visitation rights for weekends and vacations. When you enter a new relationship, your partner rightly asks, "What's this guy doing coming over here every Friday night? What's with this visiting the puppy?"

Just recently on the news, there was a story about a man suing over a dog after a breakup. I understand that people get attached to their dogs—I know I do. But you can't cut the dog in half. The person who usually takes the dog is the one that's been taking care of the dog. That doesn't mean that she bought the dog, but she's the primary caretaker, the one who's bonded with it. I once told a guy, "Go buy your own cocker spaniel. Her husband doesn't want to see you every other Saturday and Sunday picking up and returning the dog. The dog is going to live for fifteen years. Get another dog."

Bonnie's test-drive

Bonnie advised her daughters that a test-drive has its limits.

"My husband and I didn't live together before marriage, but we now have two daughters and my advice to them is, you can try it, but if you don't have

a ring on your finger and a date set by the end of a year, get out because he isn't going to commit. Don't intermingle your finances, but go for a test-drive to see if it will work. Don't hang on for more than a year for something that may never happen. Sorry, but if he isn't willing to make that leap into marriage after a year, he's obviously just waiting for something (or someone) better to come along. It's time to find someone who is willing to commit."

Judge Judy says: Bonnie gave her daughter sound advice. While kids don't always listen, keep the good advice coming. If you fail, at least you'll be able to say, "I told you so." (Just kidding!)

Lisa: No plan B

"My husband and I (married nineteen years now) lived together for a year while we planned our wedding. Looking back, we realize it wasn't the best thing to do, but by the grace of God it lasted. The reason it worked is because we were already committed as if we were married. There was no plan B. I don't understand why people would sell themselves short and give their all to someone who is not committed to them for life. Either you're committed or you're not; there's no opting out down the line if XYZ happens."

Judge Judy says: Actually, there *is* opting out in a marriage. It's called divorce. With rules, laws, courts, judges all in place to help negotiate the process. Living together is tricky.

Another word about commitment. I always tell people: ring first, joint later. By *ring* I mean wedding, not engagement. I had a woman on my show trying to get reimbursed for her engagement ring. When they picked it out, her boyfriend was strapped for cash, or he forgot to bring his wallet that day—some excuse—so she plunked down $4,000 on the promise that her boyfriend would pay her back. Instead he took off and hocked the ring.

Beware. Engagement can be a game. I know guys who figured they'd put off commitment by giving their women the ring so they can say, "Now we're engaged." As their ecstatic mates ooh and ahh over the sparkles, the men start prevaricating: "We don't have to set a date right away. Let's *enjoy* the engagement. I've proved my commitment with a ring. You're my fiancée." One couple I'm acquainted with has been engaged for nine years!

Amanda found herself in a similar dilemma.

Amanda's long engagement

"I always told my boyfriend I wouldn't live with him until we were engaged. I was ecstatic when he gave me a ring and asked me to marry him. We decided to wait a few months to set a date, but we did move in together. That was eighteen months ago. Every time I approach the subject of planning the

wedding, he gets angry and defensive and asks why I'm putting so much pressure on him. I'm so frustrated I'm thinking about calling the whole thing off. I suspect that the engagement was a ruse to get what he wanted. The other day I said to him, 'Get off the pot,' and he replied, 'I've given you everything you asked for. What more do you want from me?' I realize it's time for me to get wise, but I really do love him."

Judge Judy says: Engagement is defined as a formal agreement to get married. It's synonymous with betrothal, and it has a great deal of social meaning. Saying "yes" implies exclusivity and a journey that ends at the altar. But as the proverb goes, "There's many a slip twixt the cup and the lip," so if an engagement lingers on long after an appropriate period has passed, it's no longer an engagement—and it may become a *dis*engagement.

Wendy's nest

We can't always predict what will happen in life, even if we do everything "by the book." That's what Wendy learned.

"I am forty-five years old, born and raised in southern California and still live there. I dated and married my high school sweetheart and we were together for over twenty-five years. We did everything by the book, in the right order: dated five years, waited for marriage, moved in together, had children,

etc. We had two sons, a beautiful home, great careers, and countless friends. Life was grand! At forty years old, my husband was diagnosed with terminal colorectal cancer and died three years later. My two sons and I had our world turned upside down. Never in my wildest dreams did I think "trying again" would look like what it is today. Today I am engaged to a wonderful man who is nineteen years younger than I am. When he proposed, he wanted to move in together, have a baby together, and of course get married when I was ready. It took a lot for me to accept a new perspective of someone committing to my boys and me without being married. So I am trying again, and being open to a different way."

Judge Judy says: I believe that marriage is not just a piece of paper. It is a statement to the world that you are a legal unit. If it doesn't work, you can dissolve the unit—often a painful process. Is it better to give living together a trial run? Maybe it will work out, maybe it won't. They put erasers on pencils for a reason.

It's reasonable, considering the statistics about marriage, that you be prepared. Think of it this way. Imagine that you're considering buying a house on the beach in Malibu. And you know that there is a 50 percent chance that the beach is going to erode in front of your house. Do you spend the money to buy it, or maybe just rent a house? Most people buy, just like most people marry. They take a chance. In exchange for marrying, people have a system in place—thousands of pages of statutes—so you know where you stand if the "beach" erodes.

Personally, I would rather have a five-year marriage that ended up not working than a five-year living-together arrangement that ended up not working, because I'd have protections that don't exist outside of marriage.

We are all hopeful, but I think that because divorce has become the norm—at least half the time—few of us are in families where there is not divorce. We see that people move on after divorce. Sometimes they have other children. Sometimes they have other long-term relationships. But they survive, just like most people survive after their mates die. They may cry, "I can't live without him. I can't live without her. I'm going to dig a grave next to him and throw myself in." Six months later they're on Match.com, or booking a spot on an around-the-world singles cruise. That's a positive thing. That's a wonderful thing. Yes, we have hope. But get protection, and know what your expectations are.

My grandson Casey is engaged to Olivia, a wonderful girl. They are happily living together and planning their wedding in a year's time. Olivia said, "I wouldn't have lived with him if we weren't engaged first." Casey agreed, adding, "I don't want to deal with somebody's crap unless I'm going to marry her."

Chapter 4: Common Sense
Is Not Common

In love and life, sometimes it just boils down to common sense, which, as Will Rogers pointed out, is *not* common.

Let's talk about some insurance for those folks who just want to live together. Contrary to what many people think, there is nothing cold about sitting down and drawing up a contract before moving in together. It's both wise and realistic. It's being proactive. When two people get married, state and federal law automatically grant rights and impose obligations on each partner. When an unmarried couple is in a committed relationship, however, the law is silent. Even beyond the legal considerations, though, having this conversation about ways and means will give you important insights about your partner's views and attitudes.

Here are some of the things that should be considered for inclusion:

1. Income: Is income yours individually, or is it shared? What are the joint expenses? Who pays for what?

2. Property: Which property predates your arrangement and belongs to you as individuals? Which property was procured as a couple? Include property received as a gift or inheritance and spell out whom it belongs to in the event of the end of your relationship. Also include cars you both use.

3. Debt: If you own property jointly (a no-no in my book), how is it split? Who is responsible for paying credit-card debt in the event of the end of your relationship? Be specific! Consider your individual contributions. For example, if one of you paid 60 percent of a down payment and the other person paid 40 percent, that should be your share. Be aware, though, that jointly acquired debt is the responsibility of each party. If your partner heads for the hills, you'll be stuck with the whole enchilada. This is also the place to discuss debt incurred by you individually before the relationship. Spell it out if one partner has prior credit-card or property debt, child support, etc. You might wonder why this is relevant if you're not sharing expenses, but it is *very* relevant if your partner is so overcommitted that he or she will have problems fulfilling their end of your bargain.

4. Rent/lease: If both of your names are on the lease, you are jointly and individually responsible for payments. The same holds true for utilities, insurance, and other payments. Put in writing your agreement about how these expenses should be divided. In the event of a breakup, determine if one or the other has the right to remain in the house or apartment and take over the lease, but be sure to check with your landlord and get a written agreement. Be prepared for the

landlord to still consider both parties responsible, even if you've made a separate agreement with each other.

5. Household stuff: Granted, it gets mushier when you're talking about things like furniture or appliances—sofas, dining room sets, TVs, microwaves, leaf blowers, coffeemakers, etc. But believe me, I've had people in my courtroom arguing passionately about their right to the sofa. Best to be prepared.

6. Bank accounts: If you share an account for common expenses, spell out how the contributions are to be made, and how the account should be maintained. Keep in mind that either party can withdraw money from a joint account, and no court in the land will protect you if there's a dispute. It may make sense to have an account for everyday expenses, but enter into it with your eyes open, and try to limit the amount of money in the account to monthly needs.

When a couple enters into a living-together arrangement, each person gives something up—and hopefully gets something important in return. You're committing yourself emotionally, and there's probably some financial component—although you know my views on that.

I recommend having a written agreement for a very simple reason: people who split up tend to have grievances. Sometimes they don't think clearly. Usually they're not calling each other "sweetheart" anymore. Maybe they're enemies. Maybe they want revenge. You get the picture. So it's nice to have the written shield, and a way of putting permanent closure to your relationship.

If you're not sure you need one, let me give you a picture of what can happen, using a common example:

Jack and Jill are planning to set up an apartment. The lease will be in both names; however, should the relationship fail prior to the termination of the lease, Jill will retain the apartment and take over full responsibility for the rent. Jack will find a new apartment. Now, between the landlord and Jack, that's not a binding contract. But between Jack and Jill it may be a binding contract. So the landlord may go against Jack if Jill doesn't pay the rent. But Jack can sue Jill for the rent because of the contract. Is your head spinning? It's complicated.

I've noticed that many couples are not two-process thinkers. They avoid the potential consequences of a breakup. It may not feel romantic to think through the implications of your relationship not lasting, but that's what you have to do.

I often advise live-ins to split all the expenses. But I'm aware that people don't want to be in a situation where every day they're nickel-and-diming—"Here's my five dollars and here's your four seventy... you owe me thirty cents." It's demeaning. People want to feel there's a generosity of spirit to their living-together arrangement; they don't want to write down in the logbook every single penny that gets spent. Maybe the solution is a joint entertainment account.

Being smart doesn't have to mean being cheap and unpleasant. Enjoy your life, but plan ahead.

By the way, there seems to be a common misconception that if you live together long enough, a magical status called "common-law marriage" occurs. I often hear from people who assume that a kind of pro forma marriage kicks in after they've been together for a certain number of years. Common-law marriage is not common in the United States. It exists in nine states and there are very specific rules. Furthermore, the assumption that you are married by common law begs the question, why not get married the old-fashioned way?

I know a woman who got the ultimate kiss-off. She and her partner had been living together for years, and one day he came home from a business trip and said, "I met Yolanda. She's the one I want, and she's a great personal trainer." (With his body, he needed two!) His long-term, long-suffering partner was crushed. He promised to continue taking care of her, but she was smart enough to know that his generosity would only last until Yolanda got annoyed.

Here she was, in her midfifties, back in the game. She Botoxed, sculpted, extensioned—and still said, "What really infuriates me is that I've blown my chance. Even some overweight, balding seventy-five-year-old guy is looking for a thirty-something, and depending on his wallet, he'll probably be successful." Joan Rivers was thinking about situations like this one when she observed, "A girl, you're thirty years old, you're not married—you're an old maid. A man, he's ninety years old, he's not married—he's a catch."

The lesson here is that women have to protect themselves. They should spell out the parameters of what they're prepared to do. They shouldn't linger too long in the gray area of living together. Beware the man who says, "What's the rush?" Beware the man who says, "It's just a piece of paper." Beware the man with the hot, young personal trainer.

Mary's P.A. system

My motto is, "Be prepared." Mary's story illustrates the wisdom of that.

"One of the many pieces of advice my mother gave me throughout life was 'plan ahead'—or as we called it, P.A. Once I graduated from high school, I moved two thousand miles away from home to live with my boyfriend. We always kept our money separate and split the bills in half. With the advice of my mother, I always had backup money and a way to get home if things didn't work out. We eventually got married, but we kept the finances the same way— separate. In the end we had a daughter and soon divorced. There was no need for attorneys, just a mediator as we were clear as to what assets belonged to whom. I don't know if I just knew that things wouldn't work out, or if it was the one piece of advice from my mother that saved me from a nasty divorce."

Judge Judy says: Always have a backup plan. So few people have one. You take out insurance for cars, homes, and jewelry. You insure against floods and hurricanes. These calamities rarely happen, but you're ready. This is just insurance for affairs of the heart when they disappoint.

Sylvia's big mistake

Of course, all the planning in the world won't save you if you hook your fortunes to a bum—as Sylvia learned.

"Several years after a divorce and after my kids were grown and gone, I moved in with a man I cared for. At first, I paid half of everything. Then, after

coming home twice to a cold, dark house where the power had been turned off for nonpayment, I changed the deal. I would pay utilities, he would pay the mortgage. Whoever went to the store paid for the groceries. After ten years I discovered he had not filed taxes in eight years, and the government was after him. Fearing the loss of all my things, since our things were pretty much mingled, I moved out. Several months later, he lost his house for nonpayment and asked me to cosign for him to rent an apartment. I said no, but told him he could move in with me. He moved in and stayed on a platonic basis for two years, then moved out and married someone else."

Judge Judy says: This letter makes me wonder if Sylvia got together with Mr. Wonderful *after* the lights went out. He moved in. Stayed on a platonic basis for two years. Then moved out and married someone else. What was she thinking, letting him move back in with her—on a "platonic" basis? For two years? While he was busily dating someone else? There is that irrational behavior that often accompanies the need to nest. Don't settle. Find a hobby.

Vincent's not-so-loving nest

In Vincent's case, the warning signs were there from the start of his tumultuous relationship.

"Years ago, I moved into my girlfriend's family's home. In the first year of our highly charged romance, she was very giving. In the beginning of the second year, she suggested that I add my name to the mortgage, and so off we marched hand in hand to the attorney's office. In speaking with the attorney, I learned that our love nest was severely in arrears, and it would take a large sum of my savings to become an equal partner in saving her home. I needed to give the commitment some thought, but she viewed this as reluctance. In the weeks that followed, she began to be very argumentative, and any benefits that I had been accustomed to began to dwindle at an alarming rate. Needless to say, that was the beginning of the end. We never got to year three. What a pity."

Judge Judy says: When he describes his relationship as a "highly charged romance," right off the bat that's sending an alarm. The term *highly charged* does not bode well. Explosives are also highly charged. Interesting, too, is how quickly the highly charged romance seems to have run out of steam once the money from his savings account was not forthcoming. Vincent used his head. It is a lesson worth heeding. Are you listening, girls?

Protect yourself!

When death does you part—without that all-important piece of paper—you can end up with nothing.

"My brother-in-law recently passed away. He had been living with and taking care of his girlfriend for several years. Their living situation was not legally recognized. The girlfriend wanted to sell my brother-in-law's vehicle shortly after he passed. My niece and nephews let the girlfriend know she didn't have any legal rights to sell his car. They seized the vehicle the day of his death, and proceeded to claim a duplicate title to the car as soon as they obtained the certified copy of the death certificate. As of this date, my nephew has legally secured the vehicle. In this case, living together and not being married has caused problems obtaining family heirlooms, and I'm not sure if my niece and nephews will continue to have problems with the live-in girlfriend."

Judge Judy says: Maybe that's exactly the way he wanted it. If not, he could have provided for his girlfriend in the will. Sometimes seniors are reluctant to get married, because they want to protect their Social Security or their investments, so they live together. But you can always provide for a partner if you choose to do so. He didn't protect her and it probably happened because he didn't want to protect her. It seems cold, but there you have it. Maybe he figured, "Why should I care? I'll be dead." Maybe he was being passive-aggressive.

I know of a situation where a very successful businessman had a mistress for twenty-five years. Everyone in the family knew that she was his mistress. It was an open secret. Probably even his wife knew. Then his wife died, and his mistress moved in and did everything for him. He was elderly and needed someone to take care of him, and she did that. But he never married her, and she was filled with resentment until the day he died. I thought this was a sad story because she didn't get the one thing she really wanted, but she stayed around anyway. She needed to nest, even in a rotting tree.

Here is another piece of cautionary advice about the inheritance that wasn't.

Kathryn: If tragedy strikes

"If tragedy strikes and you're just living together, you are not entitled to anything unless a will has been done. I work for an estate-planning attorney and you won't believe the number of women who call whose partners have passed away. The boyfriend's family moves in and takes away his stuff. She calls hoping to be told she has rights, but there are none. Unless there's a will or she can prove she bought these items, she's not entitled to any of his stuff. She's also not entitled to Social Security upon his death or any portion of his pension. I know we all hope that nothing tragic will happen, but we can't foresee the future. Living together is all the rage—even my own daughter is doing it—but you need to be aware of the consequences if something bad happens."

Judge Judy says: "Rights" are not an emotion. They are not conferred by love.

Julie: A widow's protection

"Well, Judge Judy, you and I are the same age, so yes, I left my parents' home in a white dress. My mother even encouraged me to live with my boyfriend instead of marrying him. What an unusual woman for her time. The story, however, does not end there. Ten months into our marriage my husband died unexpectedly and quickly in front of me. Had we not been married, I would have had no right to make any decisions. I would have had no legal rights. I would have had no claim to the very tiny life insurance his workplace had provided. I would have had to comply with all of his family's wishes. As his family lived across the country, even the funeral would have been more stressful for me. Marriage at the very least provides legal protection for a spouse in difficult times such as I experienced."

Judge Judy says: She makes a valid point. However, I have heard women say, "I had the worst marriage in the world, but at least I get survivor's benefits." Who wants the worst marriage? Let me be clear. I don't think you have to be committed to a losing marriage. You don't have to be committed to being unhappy—I don't care how good the survivor's benefits are!

My maternal grandparents hated each other. They had a miserable marriage. Never saw them touch. Never saw them kiss. Never saw them show any affection whatsoever. She actually left him once, and that was in the 1930s. They hated each other, but they were married.

The ultimate payoff of their long, miserable marriage? They were buried side by side. My grandmother would have probably been happier in death to be buried in a different state. Nobody should be committed to being unhappy.

Diane: A senior's story

"I have enough sense to live on my own, but I know a very nice older woman in her late sixties who lives with an elderly man. He has many health issues—one foot in the grave and the back foot on a banana peel. This woman has been his companion for many years, and his health is failing now. He has a home that he lives in, and I am concerned that when this guy dies, this lady will be out in the street. She says he's told her that she can live there forever. Hah! There is a daughter right there, just waiting for the father to expire so she can grab that house."

Judge Judy says: Time will tell. If it was up to me, I'd tell the guy to show me the paperwork that says I have lifetime rights to the home, all legal and notarized. It's called a life estate. With the daughter "right there" waiting for the old guy to kick the bucket, I'd make damned sure I was covered in case the other foot slipped on the banana peel. Otherwise, I'd be getting out the Hefty bags and packing my stuff, ready to hit the road.

These are all cautionary tales. The point of being prepared and setting limits is to reduce the stressors. There are certain stressors you can't do anything about. If he has an ex-wife in the picture, you can't control that. If she has two kids, it's part of the deal. When Jerry and I were getting serious, I was presented with a potential stressor. His mother and his ex-mother-in-law were very good friends. They lived near each other in Florida and went out for dinner regularly. When the children visited, they all spent time together. Emotionally, I didn't like it, but I understood it. I was the new kid on the block, and they already had established relationships. I decided not to let that be a stressor. I even grew to adore his ex-mother-in-law. (Not the ex-wife, just her mother.)

Some stressors you can't control. There are other stressors that you can control. The most important stressor that you can control is financial. That's what usually gets most couples, married or single, in trouble.

How do you reduce the financial stressor for yourself in a living-together situation? You don't take a place to live that you can't afford together *or* alone. You don't lease a car together. You don't strap yourself with lavish vacations and credit-card debt. Once you are financially in the hole, unhappiness will surely follow.

There are other, nonfinancial stressors. Maybe she's close to her family and he can't stand them. Maybe she likes the air conditioner blasting and he's shivering. There are many differences between people, and the key to a good relationship is figuring out how you can accommodate them. Why else be together?

Chapter 5: Kids in the Picture

When Jerry and I fell in love, we both had children from our first marriages, and we talked a lot about how to blend our families. Initially, my former husband, Ron, was crazed at the idea of another man being in the house with his kids (and probably me). Jerry was sensitive to his concerns, so he took the bull by the horns and arranged to sit down with Ron. Jerry said, "I understand where you're coming from, but I really care about Judy and I care about your children. Wouldn't you prefer to have me than a guy who didn't feel this way?" Ron still wasn't thrilled, but he respected the honesty. To this day he and Jerry have a cordial relationship, but there's no question that kids complicate the picture.

When two adults decide they want to take their relationship to the next step and move in together, fine. When a child is involved, you have to be aware that you're affecting an innocent young life because *you* want a romantic relationship. The child has little say in the matter. It's up to the adults to make sure there isn't upheaval and confusion—and that your own resentments don't leak out and spoil things for the child.

Shawn: New realities

If you live together with children, should you comingle your finances? Some people think so.

"Roger and I lived together for two years, and we followed all your rules. We kept all our finances separate, and each paid half of the rent and other expenses. Seven months ago I gave birth to our child. We are thrilled with our beautiful daughter, but it's becoming increasingly apparent that the rules can no longer apply. Since we have this big joint project— our daughter!—we need to have joint finances as well. Your edict to avoid comingling doesn't apply to people with kids."

Judge Judy says: Bringing kids into the mix complicates the financial structure of living together. You know I advocate not comingling funds until you're married, but how do you say, "I'll buy diapers this week, and next week it's your turn?" If you split up, who gets the car seat? My best advice is to tread carefully. If you don't already have children, wait until you're married—and never fall for the erroneous idea that a baby will fix a broken relationship.

Bill: The pregnancy trap

Pregnancy can be a big reality check, as Bill learned.

"I always made it clear to my girlfriend that I didn't want to get married. I'm happy to live with her,

but no wedding. I never pretended otherwise, and she seemed to accept it and be happy with the arrangement until she got pregnant. Then she started pressuring me to get married because it would be wrong to bring a child into an unmarried household. I feel betrayed, and it just goes to show that people don't always mean what they say."

Judge Judy says: If you're living together and sleeping together, there's always a chance that pregnancy will occur—whether you plan for it or not. There has to be a reason Bill didn't want to get married. Personally, I'd rather be a single mother than be married to someone who doesn't want to be married to me. I don't think Bill should be pressured into getting married, but he *will* be a father for life.

Carol: What's in a name?

I have met many people whose grievances with their exes invade their current relationships. Not all parents have the best interests of their children at heart, as Carol found.

"My ex-husband has equal time with our daughter, who is five. It drives me nuts when she returns home and tells me what she has done with Daddy and 'Mommy Christine,' who is the girlfriend of the month. I have tried to talk to my ex and tell him how hurtful it is, but he blows me off and says calling Christine 'Mommy' makes things easier. He would have a stroke if she called another man 'Daddy.' I

would never confuse her like that. Why doesn't he see that you can only have one mommy and one daddy? My next stop is the family court to limit his access."

Judge Judy says: You only have one mommy and one daddy. For me those terms were always reserved for my parents—not my in-laws or others. I think it's confusing for a child to have a mommy Monday through Thursday and a different mommy Friday through Sunday, especially when one of them is not a real mommy and may not be around in three months.

I understand that there's an emotional piece for a woman who moves in with her beloved. She wants to be incorporated into his whole life. She may feel and even say, "I'd like to be like a mother to this wonderful child." It's a way of casting out that great net that women are so good at doing. It's wrong, though. It's not the behavior of a grown-up who has the best interests of a child at heart.

Besides, I don't know a man who would tolerate it. Most men would probably want to strangle the guy if their child came home and said, "Daddy Henry took me to the movies."

Having said that, if the ex refuses to see Carol's point of view, family court is not the next step. This is not a game changer.

Brenda's stress

In Brenda's case, the stress and loneliness of being a single parent led her to question what kind of relationship would work for her.

"I am a single mom with two teenage children, and I finally got out of an abusive marriage. I work two jobs to support my family, and while I would like to have some romance, I would not consider remarriage or a live-in relationship until my kids are off to college or living on their own. Too many of the women I know have nothing but stress when they allow a man to move in. Let him keep his own apartment, visit me on the weekend, and have some romance with none of the drama."

Judge Judy says: In my experience, there is a lot of additional stress when a parent allows another adult to move in, especially when the children are teenagers. Do you care for each other enough to feel that the benefits outweigh the downsides? Looking back, if I was a single mother with teenage children, I'd want the romance, too—at a separate location!

I knew a couple who lived in a very exclusive building in New Jersey, right across the river from Manhattan. They were together for many years. She was an elevator ride away. They had date nights, traveled together, and enjoyed each other enormously. When her adult children and grandchildren came to visit, they stayed with her and he popped in to say hello. When his children and grandchildren came to visit, they stayed with him and she popped in to say hello. They were the happiest couple I've ever known. They found the perfect recipe for them. The point is, there's nothing magical or sacred about living together.

Karen tiptoes back to dating

"After finally leaving an abusive marriage of twenty years, the last thing I had on my mind was a man. But after two years of celibacy, it was actually one of my sons who urged me back into the dating scene. He said, 'We're not gonna be around forever, Ma. Get your sexy butt out there!' I was mortified, not to mention a bit scared. After a few duds, I did meet what I thought was a great guy. But I always had my children and their needs in the back of my mind and didn't even entertain the idea of introducing them to him until we had been together over a year. They were aware of him, but not forced into knowing him. They learned to trust again in part because of my consideration of them in this. Things didn't work out, but it had its benefits. My children learned to accept that I am a person, not just their mother. They learned that I too have needs, emotional and otherwise, and that they can trust me not to forget them in the process of finding my happiness. They saw that they do, and always will, come first."

Judge Judy says: Karen raises a valid point. Parents are people, too. She had the right to find contentment as a woman and an individual, and she did it the right way, putting her children first. Here's another story from a devoted mother.

Joy's controlling live-in

"I divorced when my sons were seven and nine, and my ex-husband subsequently died. I raised them alone and did a pretty good job. I never dated. When my sons were in high school, I met Sam. He was a few years older than me and was very loving and supportive. It felt wonderful to have someone I could lean on after so many years doing everything myself. My boys liked Sam, too, and after nine months we decided he would move in. Almost immediately, Sam revealed a strict, controlling side that I hadn't noticed before. He started lecturing my sons about their behavior—and believe me, they're good boys. He tried to take over all the decision making, and was extremely vocal about everything from what time we sat down to dinner to how much money we spent on food and entertainment. My sons were in rebellion, and I was angry and stressed out. The live-in experiment ended after Sam made an unkind remark about my older son's girlfriend (she was of a different religion). After that, I decided to wait until my sons were grown to get entangled. If it happened, fine. If not, I could be happy on my own. I never wanted to repeat that awful experience."

Judge Judy says: When a new person is introduced into a household, tread cautiously. Sam could not bring his carpetbag of rules into Joy's home and expect everyone to fall into line. When there are children involved, newcomers must respect the fact that they are not in a position to discipline or assert authority.

Monica's mess

Monica considered moving in with her boyfriend, even though he and his children were slobs. She thought maybe she could change them.

"My boyfriend of two years asked me to move in with him and his two young sons. I was thrilled, except for one thing. Their home was a pigsty. No one ever vacuumed and dishes were piled in the sink, towels on the bathroom floor. I knew I couldn't live like that, but when I told my boyfriend, he accused me of being too picky. I'm still trying to decide whether to move in and try to change things from the inside."

Judge Judy says: I would tell the prospective live-in lothario that I would love to move in when his house passes a health department inspection. Remember, though, that bad habits do not resolve themselves overnight. So if the place is spotless on Monday, give it a week to be sure they weren't just "staging" the house.

Paul's heartbreak

Some living-together stories involving children are truly heartbreaking. Experiences like Paul's remind us that live-in partners, and even stepparents, have no official standing and no power—just a deep emotional connection.

"When my girlfriend and I moved in together, her daughter was five years old, and we developed a close relationship. I always respected the fact I wasn't her father, but I tried to be a loving adult in her life. Nine years later, my girlfriend and I split up and I moved out. She asked me to stop contacting her daughter and told me she'd be happy if I forgot I ever knew her. This was heartbreaking to me, and her daughter was very upset. I spoke to a lawyer and learned that I had no rights. It was as if our nine-year relationship had never happened. Sometimes I wonder if I would have done things differently (not moved in with her) if I had known this hurtful outcome."

Judge Judy says: I've known many cases where couples break up after being together for many years and the teenaged children demand that they be allowed to continue some kind of relationship with the man or woman who played a central role in their lives. A live-in partner—or a stepparent, for that matter—has no legal status. However, I think this mother was being shortsighted, and her actions border on abuse. After all, she was the one who introduced Paul into her child's life. She was the one who wanted her child to love him, to become close to him—

because it made her feel good that her daughter loved the man she wanted to be with. Now, after encouraging a relationship for years, she cut it off solely because she no longer felt the same way. If you introduce another source of love to your child and then end it for your own selfish reasons, understand that you're a bad parent. It's a case of needing to love your child more than you hate your ex.

A few final words about the nest and children. Throughout the ages, women have been the nurturers, and families have been built around them. Men went off to the conquests—to take Greece, take Rome, take whatever, and women stayed home and took care of the family. Women's need to nest is nature's way of making sure we continue to procreate. To be blunt about it, men have a need to get laid, and if they can create a family at the same time, that's great. If they can do it with somebody that they care about and love, that's terrific. Not all men are that interested in the nurturing part of child raising, however—especially if it's someone else's children. I know couples who have successful second and third marriages, but the man would not move in until the woman's children were on their own. As one man put it, "I don't want to parent any more children. When Sean goes away to college, we'll move in together, but until then, let's keep the romance." I can respect that point of view. People with children need to be realistic.

Chapter 6: What's Mine Is (NOT) Yours

I often get letters and e-mails like this one from a proud mother: "You've been on the air so long that my daughter grew up with you. She watched you from the time she was eight. She just started living with her boyfriend, and he said, 'The first thing we should do is get a joint bank account.' My daughter said to him, 'Are you kidding? I've been watching *Judge Judy* now for fifteen years. I don't *do* joint bank accounts.'"

I am gratified that young women are learning from me. Some people think that buying things jointly or owning property together is proof of love and commitment. But all it proves is that the stuff you purchase may not be yours.

Ownership becomes less obvious when you've comingled funds to buy something. You don't buy a joint dog. You don't get a joint cat. You don't buy a joint car. You don't buy a joint summer house. You don't buy a joint time-share. When you're just testing the waters, you don't buy a joint *anything*.

I had a case in court where Greg was suing his ex-girlfriend Charlene for her share of the time-share. Charlene said, "I don't use the time-share anymore.

He takes his girlfriends there. I'm not going to pay for his shack-ups."

His position was, "We agreed to buy a time-share, so she owes me her half."

I asked him, "Do you actually expect her to pay the maintenance on this time-share while you're there with Katrina?" He sure did! Not in my world. The problem is that Charlene remained liable until Greg sold the property. So while I may have said, "I'm not giving you any money, pal," the company that owns the condo has two names, not one, listed as owners, and Charlene remains legally liable to the company.

Samantha and the unemployed boyfriend

You can't squeeze blood out of a turnip, and unless your mate has a trust fund, you're going to be paying the bills if he's unemployed. Samantha failed to consider this.

"I dated this guy for about a year and we lived together, too. Of course, he wasn't employed, and I was the only one with an income. Naturally, I paid for everything. At first I didn't mind, but after a while, it seemed that he pretty much expected me to pay. It got to the point where he didn't even ask if I'd buy him something, and I didn't like doing it because I couldn't afford it. Eventually, the relationship just fizzled away. As a result of this and some other bad relationships, I have set ground rules for whom I date. First of all, he must be employed or have his own income. Secondly, he must not be living with a parent

or with anyone else who is supporting him. And, third, he must have his own car or truck (no bicycles). If he meets all three of these requirements, then being trustworthy, drug-free, nondrinking, and a good companion are also important."

Judge Judy says: Samantha learned her lesson, but I found her description interesting. Notice that she said, "*Of course*, he wasn't employed... *Naturally*, I paid for everything." There's no "of course" or "naturally" about it. If you can't trust your heart, use your brain, your eyes, and your ears. And hide your checkbook. Often people make the mistake of ignoring objective data at the beginning of a relationship. They think they have to let time make the big reveal about the true person. They ignore the clues that are glaringly present from the start about trustworthiness, alcohol use, behavior, and finances. (Joan Rivers also wisely advised, "Never floss with a stranger.")

My court is crowded with people—most often women—who loan money to boyfriends without any concrete agreement about getting paid back. As one of these women explained to me, "The bank wouldn't loan him the money, so I agreed." To which I replied, "What are you, the Bank of Stupid?" Here's the big question: If you marry or stay together, would you expect to be repaid? If not, it's not really a contract, it's an investment in the future. People come to my courtroom and say, in effect, "I invested in you with the expectation that we were going to be together. I should get some compensation."

In my experience, people living together don't sit down on the bed at the end of the day and discuss the payment plan for the $3,000 one loaned the other for his or her business: "I'll pay $250 a month, with x interest... thank you very much, turn off the lights and roll over, baby." That isn't the way it happens. If it doesn't make sense to the fact finder—the judge— it's usually not true.

I've noticed a strange phenomenon: when people are together, it's a gift. When they break up, it's a loan. Let me ask you: How many people do you know who can afford to give a $12,000 car as a gift to a stranger? People who are in LOOOVE, that's who. As the great sage Lily Tomlin once said, "If love is the answer, could you rephrase the question?"

Amber's property mistake

Amber made the common mistake of getting enmeshed, and then went on to make things worse.

"I recently separated from a year-and-a-half-long relationship. We shared an apartment, checking and savings accounts, and pretty much everything else. We were not married. Our relationship became very destructive and we wasted a lot of time and resources in the long run. One time a fight resulted in me leaving, and I took the TV and Xbox with me and sold them at a pawnshop. He could do nothing about it because it was considered common property. We

ended up returning the check for the sale, getting the items back, and continuing our relationship. Not too long after, we separated again and I had no way of getting money from our joint accounts because they were in his name. Now we are in a whole new harassment battle, but that is for another time. Will I do that again? Absolutely not, and neither should anyone else."

Judge Judy says: Half of nothing is nothing. A "joint" account in *his* name is not yours. It's his. If you deposit *your* money into *his* account, it becomes *his* money.

Here's another story about bank-account shenanigans.

Barry's sneaky deal

"Because of problems with my ex-wife's unreasonable child support demands, I used my live-in girlfriend's bank account to deposit my paychecks. I never anticipated a problem, but when we separated and I was forced to move out, she refused to give me the money that was rightfully mine. It just happened to be in her bank account. The bank said I had no recourse, even though she was holding my money hostage. Live and learn, but it was a raw deal."

Judge Judy says: If it's in her account, it's her money. If you went to court, you'd be asking the court to make a moral judgment. Here's the problem: you didn't do the right thing. You tried to hide assets so you could avoid your legal responsibility to pay child support. In court there's something called the doctrine of clean hands—the assumption that those coming before the court aren't trying to commit fraud. You, sir, have very dirty paws.

James: Wait until the thirtieth anniversary!

James was cautious, perhaps to a fault.

"I am a twenty-seven-year-old man and have lived with someone once. We never had a joint bank account or bought anything that was considered mutual property. When we split, it was easy to discern what was mine and what wasn't. There were no arguments about money or property division. While living together before marriage is something that's done normally today, I should say that I have no time for people who comingle their funds and pets before they are legally bound through a contract of marriage. Even when a couple is legally bound through marriage, and the relationship ends, division of property can still be messy. To be perfectly blunt, even if I was married I would still have reservations about opening a joint bank account or buying anything that would have to be divided up if the relationship fizzled. Maybe on the thirtieth anniversary, I would consider it."

Judge Judy says: James did it right—nothing joint or comingled, nothing messy, except perhaps emotions. Chances are, if he finds the right partner and marries her, he will soften on joint ownership.

Mary's housing woes

Mary did it backwards—house first, commitment later. It didn't work out so well.

"Years ago, I was in a relationship. Neither of us was ready for marriage, but we wanted a house. So we built a house together. We had verbal agreements as far as who paid what. That went fine, no problems with that. After a year, almost to the date, we broke up. Both our names were on the house. There was no equity after one year's time, and I had to move out, since I couldn't afford the mortgage and he could. He kept the house and made the payments. That was fine with me, except I wondered whether I would be owed something years later when there was equity. Years after we broke up, he asked me to sign a release so I would get nothing if the house sold. My heart sank! I never made one payment after I left, but legally I was to receive what was rightfully mine. I think I did the morally right thing: I signed. My family thinks I'm crazy, and maybe I am. But I think I did the right thing as we broke up friends after all."

Judge Judy says: You did the morally right thing, and there *is* karma in this world. If I were you, I would have done the same thing. It's classy.

I hear a few cases involving homes each year, but hundreds about cars. Here's one example: John and Julie moved in together, and since his credit was better than hers, he took out a loan for her car. They made an agreement that as long as she took care of the payments, the car was hers. Then they broke up. She got the car. He got the shaft.

I got the case in *Judge Judy*'s courtroom because John thought he should get the car back. I'm sure he expected me to agree, but I did not. Their agreement was that as long as she made the payments she could keep the car. She was making the payments. That was their contract.

He complained. "But we're not together anymore. You're saying I have to worry about this car?"

"Yes, you do." I confirmed that I did understand that Julie could stop making the payments. She could drop the collision insurance and just have the liability insurance and get in a car accident.

Julie's position was that she'd been making payments on the car for three years, and why should he get to ignore her contribution and take the car back? See how complicated it gets?

These are living-together problems. These are not marriage problems, because courts have rules regarding marital property.

Richard: Accounting errors

Richard's experience demonstrates why I don't recommend joint checking accounts.

"I was young and stupid at the time, and got a joint checking account with my live-in girlfriend. She thought if there were checks in the checkbook left to be written, any amount could be spent. Until then, I had a triple-A credit rating. After a bunch of her checks bounced, not only was our account overdrawn, but there were angry collection agents pounding at the door and ringing the phone. Nightmare. Separate everything is the way to go."

Judge Judy says: Well, I don't know how old Richard's girlfriend was. However, when I was sixteen and a half, I started college. Yes, I was precocious, but I knew nothing about accounting and financing. My father opened a checking account and gave me a checkbook. It was for emergencies.

Being a teenager, I had constant emergencies. One day I got a call from my father. He was fuming. "We just heard from the dean of students," he said. That alarmed me because I was a well-behaved young lady. If they said lights out at ten, I'd have them out at nine thirty. Well, I was writing these checks for five and ten dollars. My father had put $100 in my account. I never kept track. I was writing bad checks all over the campus, figuring as long as there were checks, there was money. But in fairness to me, I was sixteen. Age and maturity are supposed to make you smarter.

Linda's regret

A test-drive of living together might have saved Linda some grief, as long as she was paying attention to his spending habits, and assuming they didn't comingle finances.

"I wish I'd lived for at least a year with my ex-husband before marriage. Then I would have learned of his complete lack of responsibility with money. He was a nice guy, but he went through a paycheck like Sherman through Georgia. I had some inkling of his poor money management before we married, but it really came home to roost when we married and began sharing a bank account. My advice to women, married and single: if you learn your partner is a poor money manager, separate your finances, as I did, before your credit is ruined along with his. Not to sound cynical, but it also makes things easier if and when your marriage or love nest breaks up. If I had lived with this man and shared expenses, bills, and so on, I probably would have reconsidered marrying him after watching our resources slowly circling the drain. Money problems were a major part of our divorce. I am now happily single, and financially independent."

Judge Judy says: You can learn a lot from living together with a person prior to getting married. Remember what I said earlier: when you're dating, you're actually meeting a *representative* of the person. Often, it's only living together that really lets you see if they're good with all manner of things.

Finances. Cleanliness. Good at sharing. Good at acting responsibly. There are certain things you can learn if you have your eyes open going into a relationship. Sometimes you may have your eyes open and dive in despite the warning signs. It's crazy. You touch the pot and it's hot. You pick it up barehanded anyway. Who's the schmuck—you or the pot?

WHO'S THE SCHMUCK, YOU OR THE POT?

Dakota: Left with nothing

Under the guise of "saving money," Dakota's partner left her broke.

"I had a very lovely apartment. I met a nice man, we fell in love, and after two years I moved into his house. He insisted, saying it would save us money and he wanted to show our commitment to each other. I gave in, thinking our relationship was never going to end. We didn't have a contract or a discussion about

bills. We just paid them as they came up. Most months we split the mortgage. Eventually he lost his business and I had to pay the bills, including vet bills for his dog. Soon we drifted apart. I had to move out with nothing, no savings, just the clothes on my back. I lost the new living room set, bedroom set, washing machine, kitchen table, silverware, and cool kitchen utensils I bought. I should have listened to my mother when she said, 'move in only when you are married.'"

Judge Judy says: Don't invest in a stranger's house. A simply written contract defining what was his and what was yours would have saved you some of the heartache: "This is mine, that's yours." However, when you play house and it fails, most often someone gets burned.

Jen: Collection calling

Jen encountered what I call the "never-ending ex." Long after they were no longer a couple, she was reminded of him daily when the collection agents called.

"When I was eighteen, I moved in with my boyfriend. We shared a joint checking account and credit cards, and both of our names were on the apartment lease. Two years later, we broke up and I moved back in with my parents. I received a call shortly afterward from a collection agency. My ex had been using our credit cards during the last few months of our living together and not paying the bills.

He would intercept the mail so that I was unaware that there was a balance. This was before the Internet and electronic accounts. Because I was the primary on the account, they came after me. He has run up the bills to over $10,000. I took him to court and received a judgment, but you can't get blood from a stone. I never received a penny from him. I paid back my creditors, but vowed never again to share an account with anyone. Years later, when I got married, I maintained my own checking and savings accounts and credit cards. I didn't even change my last name. Girls, protect yourselves!"

Judge Judy says: Jen was eighteen, old enough to have watched my program and listened. She probably knew joint was wrong, and she went ahead. It's almost like salmon who die after they spawn. They know they're going to die, but they do it anyway.

Ladies and gentlemen, boys and girls of all ages— before you wed, joint *nothing*!

Ann's hard lesson

Sadly, "once burned, twice shy" does not apply to all situations. It took Ann two times burned to pull her hand away from the fire.

"I allowed my boyfriend (unemployed, mostly) to move in with me and we promptly ran through credit cards and all kinds of money. When I left him the first time and moved back home several states away, I lost everything. I'm ashamed to admit I didn't learn my

lesson then, and when he followed me to a different state, I actually got back together with him. Think anything different happened? It got worse—I married him. It was the worst two and a half years of my life, that marriage. I somehow got the gumption to go back to school and he disappeared, leaving me to pick up the tab for the divorce, naturally. Fortunately, we had no children or property. I take full responsibility for being a sucker."

Judge Judy says: Don't share anything except a bed until you're married. If you get in too deep, you might not be able to climb back out. Courts are not designed to deal with "almost marrieds." And they really don't want to. Keep it simple, kids.

Chapter 7: There's No Relationship Fairy

In the movie *Pretty Woman*, a man named Edward Lewis (played by Richard Gere) falls in love with Vivian, a prostitute (played by Julia Roberts). Remarkably, Vivian is still a romantic who says, "I want the fairy tale." When Richard announces that he wants to set her up in a condo, he expects her to be happy and grateful. Instead she says, "When I was a little girl, my mama used to lock me in the attic when I was bad, which was pretty often. And I would—I would pretend I was a princess... trapped in a tower by a wicked queen. And then suddenly this knight, on a white horse with these colors flying, would come charging up and draw his sword. And I would wave. And he would climb up the tower and rescue me. But never in all the time that I had this dream did the knight say to me, 'Come on, baby, I'll put you up in a great condo.'"

Vivian learned that life wasn't a fairy tale, but because this was a movie, she ended up getting her "knight." However, in the real world, there's no such thing as a relationship fairy. Couples have to work things out, set their standards, and try to find a mate who meets the most important ones.

Having standards is a good thing: he or she must be employed. Not living with a parent. Self-supporting. Must be Jewish or Catholic or Hindu. Showers daily. These are all reasonable standards. Also tall, slim, muscular, intelligent, etc. There are many variables. In Florida, the ability to drive at night ranks right up there with being housebroken.

There are also crises that come along that nobody planned for, but they land in your lap and you have to deal with them. Let's say you're happily living together and your partner loses his or her job, which happens a lot in this economy. Suddenly you're living with someone who can't contribute financially. If you love your mate, you're probably not going to kick him or her to the curb. Do you really expect to be repaid for shouldering more of the financial burden? That's usually where I come in.

I know a couple in a long-term relationship. They met when she was sixty-two and he was seventy-eight. He didn't want to get married. She accepted his decision. They lived together and had a good ten years. Then he got sick and she dumped him on his children. Would she have stayed if they were married? Probably yes. That piece of paper—that commitment—really does make a difference. Sometimes it's the logical course after a "test" period of many years.

Patti's mixed message

"I have spent twenty-one years with my man (we never actually married) and they have been a bit

traumatic at times. I kicked his sorry ass out many times for behaving badly and making poor decisions, but I can honestly say now that he is forty-five, he is just starting to figure things out and how things need to be to live with me. Our children were miserable when he was gone—they toe the line when he is around, so they do understand their boundaries because of his influence. Sometimes you've got to let them go figure out what is important. If they come back to you, they are yours to mold however you see fit. If they don't, they never were worth your time. Follow your heart and if they cheat, kick them to the curb. For that is a trust that can never be repaired."

Judge Judy says: First, why spend twenty-one years with kids and all and not be married? A test-drive should not wear out the car. Furthermore, you can never mold a forty-five-year-old. He's molded, and the mold is set.

Stacia's advice

Stacia raises a good question: Does living together "work?"

"My mother always told me, 'I would never wash a man's dirty laundry unless we were legally married. None of this living together nonsense for me.' I am sixty-four and this was a big no-no in my day. Everyone says you get to know the other person when you live together—NOT. Time and time again I have seen that one party or the other changes when they

are legally married. He gets really stingy with the money. She gets lazy and with no children yet, wants to stay home and not go to work. The divorce rate is 50 percent, so this proves living together first does not necessarily work."

Judge Judy says: Living together is now acceptable and even desirable. I don't see that changing. If you choose to be roommates with benefits, the benefits should apply to both parties—and I'm not just talking about sex. Testing the waters should be about whether you can work out all the day-to-day details of living in a responsible way.

Over the years I've observed tens of thousands of couples, and sometimes it's easier to acknowledge that men and women are basically different. Warriors are the served, not the servers. Women are the nurturers. They don't fight with the car dealer and the mechanic. They don't open the jars or fix the toilet. Of course, there are exceptions—I even know some—but not many.

Here's my theory. In order to insure the continuation of the human species God created a mechanism in most women that allows them to obliterate the pain of childbirth. Only in that way could we be assured that women would have more than one child. While I do not remember the discomfort of the delivery of any of my children, momentous events in my life, I do remember the date, time, place, and circumstance of any and every time my dear husband Jerry aggravated me. He usually plays dumb when I can pull up an ancient event and recount the conversation in colorful detail but cannot remember where we had dinner yesterday. Jerry, on the other hand, remembers the dinner. Period. My point is, when we accept the way things are, life is a lot simpler. Keep your standards but accept reality.

Morgan: A role model

"I was an old-fashioned, smart girl when it came to men. I paid my own way through college, got a great job, and saved money. My credit was perfect. I met a nice man who wanted to live with me, but not marry me. I told him to shove off—I was not going to be anybody's testing ground. I wanted to be married and have children, in that order. I refused to give away any of my power as a self-respecting woman. I also wanted to be a role model to my own children. I made a checklist of things my husband must have. They included integrity, responsibility, being educated, a moral compass, and above all, respect for women. I didn't compromise or talk myself into thinking I could change a man. I have now been married for thirty-two years and our daughters are following my path. Ladies! Don't give away your power as a woman! If you demand the best from a man, he will deliver. If not, tell him to move on and out of your life. Bad decisions have bad consequences."

Judge Judy says: I applaud Morgan for setting her standards. She was smart, organized, and lucky.

She used all the right ingredients for a good marriage, and the recipe was perfect. She served as a role model for her children. Good for her!

Sandra: Commit it or ditch it

Sandra tried marriage and she tried living together. Both relationships ended, but in only one was she protected.

"Living with someone without any legal ties can be a tragedy. I have been married, and I have lived with someone without being married. Getting divorced was no picnic—the only good thing about getting divorced is that you have the laws protecting you. In the state I live in, it's divided fifty-fifty. When I lived with someone, it was my home, and although the deal was to have him pay for some of the outstanding bills, it rarely happened. He once in a while would fix something around the house, thus making me feel like I was getting a real deal. NOT. I was fortunate in the end, because it was my home, and because he brought nothing to the party, it ended with me having everything I started with. It was basically a free ride for him. I had to make my mortgage payments; the house and everything else were in my name. The lesson learned is if you are not good enough for him to commit 100 percent, then forget about him and the relationship. He doesn't respect you as a woman or partner."

Judge Judy says: When a man's sole role is occasionally fixing things around the house, he does not a partner make. Especially when he presents himself as God's gift to home maintenance. There's more to a relationship than just getting by.

Lil: In the blink of an eye

"I blinked, and it's thirty years later. I'll be fifty this year, and we've got a fourteen-year-old entering high school. How did I let myself get here without a wedding ring? By my choice. The only marriage in my family that ever lasted was my maternal grandparents'. Till death did they part. I wasn't pushing for something that was painfully obviously not in his mind-set. Lost: my youth and girlish good looks were given to him. Gained: a nonviolent, nondrinking man; a wonderful father to our son; and a son who has both of his parents in his life. Trade-off: some might blink and say they've wasted thirty years of their life by not having a piece of paper to prove their love. I'm not blinking. We kept our finances separate and I built a house in my name only. I'm in love, but that doesn't make me blind. In four short years, our 'baby' goes off to college. If we have no further future at that point, I have a fully furnished home waiting."

Judge Judy says: Lil struck the bargain she wanted. Her life experience was happy and did not include marriage. It doesn't work for everybody, but clearly she has enjoyed and will continue to enjoy a love-blessed relationship. In the end, that's all each of us hopes for.

Chapter 8: The EX Factor

If a married couple divorces, there is an end. Property is divided, child custody is arranged. You move on, and if you're smart you don't repeat your mistake. However, living together can be the gift that keeps on giving, long after you've gone your separate ways. If you take on joint responsibilities, they have to be met, no matter what the state of your love life. And if your partner disappears or refuses to pay, you have to do it alone. I've met many people with ruined credit who are still paying off cars they no longer possess, or mortgages they're covering on their own. And not a court in the land can help them.

Marnie's hard fall

"I thought dissolving a marriage was a hassle, so the next time around, my beau and I 'just' lived together. The breakup was a mess! Joint bank account? Couldn't get him off it without his signature and he'd moved to another state! Keys to the apartment? He was still on the lease, so he could still enter. I couldn't take him off the lease without—you guessed it—his signature! He lived three hundred miles away, so imagine my shock to come home and

find him sitting on my couch. The electricity was in his name, and he turned it off one day out of the blue. I couldn't move for three months because of the lease. He didn't have a job or a pot to...you know the story. The lease was joint, so we were both responsible, but they don't go after the one without any money. Divorce stinks, but at least it ends and there is a judge to make a fair (and final) ruling."

Judge Judy says: Some people are motivated to do the right thing and be responsible. Others, not so much. This is something most sensible adults can figure out fairly quickly in a relationship—maybe even on a first date when he leaves his wallet at home.

Megan: Rebound error

The period after divorce can be difficult, and sometimes people are particularly vulnerable. That was the case with Megan. She divorced a husband and found a moocher.

"After my divorce I met a man who I thought had my best interests at heart. He had just left one job and was looking for another. During that time he moved in with me and I was happy, but we made the mistake of not discussing the financial arrangement beforehand. Six months later he only had a part-time job and would not contribute to any household expenses. His explanation? Since I had my place before we moved in, he was not causing any extra expenses. He bought food he liked to eat and thought

that was enough. Didn't he enjoy a warm shower, heat, a dry roof over his head? It was decision time, and I gave him thirty days to come up with some cash to contribute. He actually said I would have to have him evicted because he now had residency. Yikes! This was a person with some very bad intentions to take advantage of me."

Judge Judy says: It always amazes me that the people who can't find a job—*ever*—are so well versed in their rights. I had a case recently in court. They were divorced, but she took pity on him because he had no place to stay and he promised to help around the house. She let him sleep on the couch, thinking it would be a short-term deal. But now she couldn't get rid of him. He came to my courtroom with the claim that he had *established residency*. This prince couldn't get a full-time job, but the residency requirement he understood. You can't make these things up.

Sally: For all intents and purposes

Sally liked to say that for all intents and purposes, they were married. She found out otherwise.

"I lived with my former boyfriend for thirteen years. I used to say, 'For all intents and purposes, it's a marriage.' But I was wrong, because when things started to deteriorate, we did not have the impetus to fight as hard to save the marriage...because we had no marriage to save. Ours wasn't even an atypical

story. I was quite slender when we first got together, but the last three years of our relationship, I put on weight, and it greatly affected our intimacy. I'm sure this often happens to couples who have been together a long time. But when you don't have that life commitment that comes with marriage, it is so much easier to say, well, we're really just friends at this point, so let's break up. It was tragic. It's been two years since the breakup, and I realize that we should have fought to save the relationship. I get it now. Marriage is not just a piece of paper. It is a commitment to work through things and not just take the easy way out."

Judge Judy says: Sally is right. I agree that when there is a marriage, people work harder to resolve the issues in an attempt to improve and save it. My question to Sally would be: if she knew her weight gain affected their intimacy, why didn't she work at changing it?

Jerry and I have been together thirty-seven years. He has never seen me without my face washed, a little gloss on my lips. I get up in the morning and I'm out of that bedroom into the bathroom to put myself marginally together. Why would I want him to see me at less than my best? I expect the same from him. We're no longer young, but the two of us enjoy seeing each other look the best we can be. I don't buy the idea that people should just accept their partners the way they are no matter what. Would you accept a partner who announced, "I don't want to work anymore. I'm just going to play golf?" No. You'd say,

"I came into this relationship with the expectation that you would work." You'd have every right to say, "This is not what I bargained for." This guy has every right to say he didn't bargain for a mate who weighed eighty pounds more than when he met and fell in love with her. There's nothing superficial about that.

LADIES, THIS IS A <u>BIG</u> MISTAKE!

Since, sadly, most live-in relationships don't pan out, at least we should be smart enough to learn from the experience—store the information in your brain under "Mistakes Not to Make Again."

Frogs don't become princes. Check.

Once a bum, always a bum. Check.

A leopard doesn't change its spots. Check.

If he fell in love with Twiggy, he may not care for Mama Cass. Check.

Chapter 9: The Art of Cohabiting

My grandmother was a repository of all Yiddish quotes, which if strictly followed were designed to ensure a happy life. She was, of course, miserable with her own mate. However, as I age, so many of those sayings resonate with truth, such as, "If you charge nothing, you'll get a lot of customers." That pearl of wisdom seemed old-fashioned at the time, but it still applies today. I learned to value myself and not to rely on anyone else for my worth. I'm a judge, not a moral arbiter, but I've seen enough in my courtroom to understand that a lack of self-esteem is at the heart of most screwups. The fear of being alone, the belief that they're not good enough, the lack of self-worth, all cause people to get involved in destructive relationships.

I wish there was a law that men and women could only join together when both of them are emotionally intact individually. If you are dependent on another human being to make you happy, that's not the same thing as being happier in the company of that person. I personally would not be as happy without my partner. I would have friends, a career, children, and grandchildren, but I am happier being part of a couple with all its ups and downs. I know Jerry feels the same way. Together we are better than separate.

People who know our story are aware that Jerry and I once got divorced after we'd been together for twelve years. We were both independent people. We were judges. We were happy being independent. However, we discovered that we were not as happy as we were being together. There was something missing, and that's why we remarried. We weren't thinking, "I can't live without you." We were thinking, "I can live better *with* you." A whole person, capable and independent, is sure to be a better mate.

Here are some stories of people who learned the art of living together.

Kay: Straight talking

"We have lived together for thirty-four years this month. We say we have a learner's permit. From the very beginning we have kept everything separate. I've never loaned him money nor has he loaned me money. When we were both working and decided to move in together, the arrangement was that he paid the mortgage (because it was his home) and housing association dues. I paid the utility, grocery, and liquor bills. It worked. Now after thirty-four years we have bought a townhouse together in joint tenancy with both our names on the deed and mortgage. He has two children and I have none. Once a year we have a family sit-down and discuss any changes that they should know about. We have wills, HIPPA forms, and health care powers of attorney."

Judge Judy says: Kay and her partner did all they could to protect themselves. They clearly communicate well. Although she didn't explain why they never married, it seems to have worked for them so far. I hope their legal documents include a plan if their relationship goes south.

If you're going to live together and do these things together, don't think a verbal agreement is enough. I know a woman who even put the gifts in writing. On the receipt it said: "Gift, sweetheart. This was your Teflon-coated snow shovel. Happy anniversary."

I appreciate that Kay and her partner communicate openly and include the kids in the discussions so there are fewer misunderstandings. A generation ago, women kept quiet and kept the peace. If they needed a new dress for an event, they wouldn't discuss it because chances are he'd say, "We can't afford it." They'd just go out and buy the dress, and when he asked about it, they'd laugh and say, "*This* old thing?"

But as I said, it's great to be able to have adult discussions. If I'd had the courage to have these discussions another civilization ago, when I first married, that would have been wonderful. The only discussion I remember was with whom we were going to spend Thanksgiving. Actually, that's a pretty funny story.

My first husband's mother was a very nice lady, and she had a best friend, whose last name was Aaron. One year they would make Thanksgiving and have the Aarons, and the next year the Aarons would make Thanksgiving and have the Levy family. They had been doing that for twenty-some years, ever since their children were little.

We got married in December, and had spent that prior Thanksgiving with his parents. My parents rightly thought that we would celebrate the next year with them. My husband said, "No, our family tradition is that we celebrate Thanksgiving together with the Aarons every year."

I was frustrated, but my father got on the phone with my mother-in-law. She carefully explained the family tradition. My father, God love him, replied, "Eve, you're not rich enough to have traditions." That was the end of that.

Amy's easy way

"I couldn't agree more that cohabitants should keep everything separate. I lived with my ex-boyfriend for a year. During that time we had separate everything, from bank accounts all the way down to kitchen gadgets. When he moved out, I wanted to keep the drapes that fit the front bay window perfectly. I traded with him for the popcorn maker that someone had given to us as a gift. Worked out perfectly and we were both whole and happy."

Judge Judy says: Good for you—although that was one expensive popcorn maker.

Diane's simple equation

"If you can't trust him with your heart, don't trust him with your money. I don't understand these comments from people saying they will live together and never get married. If you can't trust each other enough to make a commitment in writing before the state, do you really want to trust this person to have access to your belongings, finances, and body? Marriage is the legal way to protect yourself from ruin if the relationship doesn't work out."

Judge Judy says: I, too, am old-fashioned enough to appreciate the concept of marriage as a lifestyle. I think it's a good investment if you love your mate and are prepared to work at it. Marriages don't flourish without some tender gardening. It's a mistake thinking that all you need is love. Love is only the start.

Beverly's smart gift

"When my washer and dryer weren't working so well, my boyfriend bought me a new set as a gift. I asked him to indicate that it was a gift to me on the receipt and give the receipt to me. We will likely do things like this indefinitely so there is never any confusion."

Judge Judy says: Very sweet—as long as he doesn't expect you to do his laundry.

Laura dots the i's and crosses the t's

"I agree that people who live together should keep finances separate. However, there should be clear communication regarding expectations of spending, money owed for bills, rent, transportation, etc. I moved in with my boyfriend after dating for four months. I knew we would get married, but even now, we maintain our own separate bank accounts and credit cards. We have always communicated to each other about how we are spending our own money, and have always split our mutual living expenses. We discussed this arrangement in detail before deciding to move in together. I feel that this step is crucial in this situation. Not only discussing where your money is going to be spent, but more importantly, discussing current debt, assets, and expectations of each other and how things would be divided in the event of separation. If you aren't comfortable discussing these things, then you should not move in with each other. They can lead to problems in and outside of the relationship."

Judge Judy says: Nobody likes to talk about the unglamorous parts of living together. However, at some point rent, utilities, vacations, and food all must be paid for. Having the discussions from the beginning is the right way.

Richard: It's a matter of respect

"Living in a state where marriage isn't an option (yet!), we don't have much of a choice. My first job was at a bank, and I learned early on through others' mistakes that joint accounts are a bad idea, even when you're married. We own our home together, but everything else is separate. We chose to split the bills evenly, even though we have different salaries. The one who handles the money best handles the shared bills. Adult responsibilities come first, and anything else waits unless one or both of us has the money to indulge. If you go into a relationship with reasonable expectations that you can agree on and live with, you can make it work, married or not. If you aren't married, there are other ways to set up legal arrangements for the things that matter most. Don't be afraid to use them. WWJS? First and foremost, if you can't respect and trust your partner or spouse, you don't have any business living together in the first place."

Judge Judy says: Richard is right on all counts. He figured out a perfectly sane financial arrangement with his mate. The fact that it works is a testament to respect and shared values.

Sheila: Survivor's wisdom

"I will start by saying I never would have moved in or made children with a man who wasn't married to me. But that's just me. And if you think the benefits

are just in marriage, you may be wrong. I am a thirty-one-year-old woman with five little girls who became a widow five months ago. It is the all-consuming thought every second of my life at this point. Even as a widow, I am much better off than the women who played house with their significant others. I qualify for worker's compensation for both me and my children; unmarried, you do not. I inherit the property of the marriage as his surviving spouse. You cannot imagine the horror stories I've heard from women over the past five months who never got married but were clearly the significant person for many years in that man's life. How can you prove legally that you deserve to be treated as his spouse if you weren't legally married? There are many more things to consider! Also, imagine you were to die and he had to survive. ..."

Judge Judy says: Sheila is quite correct. The legal benefits of being married often far outweigh the drawbacks.

Tracie: Sometimes there's a miracle (but don't count on it)

"I am now forty-six years old. I met my husband in 1990 and we moved in after six months of dating. We had our first child in 1992 and our second in 1997. We had both been married before and although my husband asked me several times to marry him, I liked our relationship the way it was. Neither of us had an agenda (any type of assistance) or ulterior

motive to stay unwed. We were content, and our children had both Mom and Dad in a happy home. We bought a home in 1997, acquired many assets through the years, and have joint accounts, all without the benefit of marriage. We made wills, POAs, HCPs, etc., to ensure we and our children would be protected. Sure, we have had our struggles, but we chose to work through them even though either of us could have walked away because there's no marriage license. After twenty years together, we married two years ago with our two children as witnesses! We may certainly be the exception to the rule, but I wouldn't have changed anything about these past twenty-two years."

Judge Judy says: There is always that atypical experience that doesn't fit the four corners of any logical argument. If it worked for twenty years, why marry?

Kerry: In writing

"My partner and I have been together for thirty-two years. Our agreement has always been that what we are able to contribute to the household monetarily represents the percentage we hold. For many years I had a job with a nonprofit organization and only earned a minimum wage. My partner was fortunate to have a high-paying job. I was able to contribute 40 percent and he did 60 percent. We had a lawyer do the paperwork and set up a trust for the nieces and nephews based on that. Putting it in writing up front

and expressing our desires with family has allowed us to relax and enjoy life together."

Judge Judy says: Good communication, logical thinking, and mutual respect worked for Kerry and her partner, but when it comes to living together, stories like Kerry's are not the norm.

Erin: No party, please

"*I have been living with my best friend/boyfriend for eighteen years. We have paid off the house and cars and any debt. The reason we are not getting married is because people will think we need to throw a party after, or go on a honeymoon or buy rings. Which all cost money. We would rather use the money to help homeless animals or for retirement. God knows the story and he knows what we are using the extra money for. I think he is okay with it.*"

Judge Judy says: If it works, fine. Me, I'd spring for the license.

Amanda: Ode to nice guys

"*A friend of mine moved in with her boyfriend. Things didn't exactly work out, but they had both paid for the apartment. They couldn't figure out who would get the apartment, but her boyfriend had a higher-paying job than she did. He was so kind throughout the entire thing and actually told her she could keep it. They were both mature about splitting up the furniture and such when he moved out. I was surprised that two people so young could figure things out on their own without fighting about it. When I asked him what made him let her have the apartment he said, 'My dad raised me to be a gentleman and I know she doesn't make as much as I do, so I decided to do the right thing and let her have it. We cared about each other at some point and just because we aren't together anymore doesn't mean I have to be a Bleep.' I was shocked and amazed that men like that still exist, because I've seen people fight tooth and nail over a cup and saucer."*

Judge Judy says: Amanda reminds us that there are good guys and good gals out there. Maybe more good than bad. I see plenty of the other kind in my courtroom, but this can be a lesson to everyone who enters into a relationship: be kind and be fair. It's good karma.

Chapter 10: There Ought to Be a Law

We have created an entire court system for people who marry and divorce, and that system is pretty busy. People who want a legal remedy because they decided to try out living together are out of luck. There is no court for them. Should there be?

I don't write the laws, but if I did, they'd probably look something like the following. Consider them the basis for a living-together contract. I guarantee if you establish these limits at the outset, you won't be seeking justice from an unresponsive court system later.

 ❖ Our live-in arrangement, by which we test the waters prior to marriage, shall only be in place for one year. If at the end of that year we have not become officially engaged and set a date for the wedding, the arrangement shall end.

 ❖ During our trial living-together period, we shall not jointly purchase or procure a house, a car, a boat, a cell-phone plan, a credit card, a health-club membership, or any other big-ticket item. Nor shall we jointly adopt a dog, a cat, a parrot, or an iguana.

❖ The cost of renting a common domicile shall not exceed either person's ability to pay the entire sum. Both names shall be on the lease, with a written agreement about who gets the place if there is a breakup.

❖ All loans shall be memorialized in a contract. Otherwise they will be considered gifts.

❖ All expenses shall be divided equally, and a full written record shall be maintained.

❖ If during the course of the trial arrangement, circumstances change—a lost job, an illness, a move—a new contract shall be written that addresses the revised reality.

If your partner balks at signing off on any of these simple, smart rules, run for the hills. Avoid years and even decades of regret. As the saying goes, "If you lie down with dogs, you'll wake up with fleas."

Conclusion: Imperfect Unions

Here is a final caveat. In any relationship, there are imperfections. Jerry and I continue to have a great run, in spite of the fact that he has developed some idiosyncratic behaviors over the years that I find quite irritating. I have no idiosyncratic behaviors that I'm aware of. In fact, I asked Jerry,

"If I had the same shtick you have, would we still be together?" He replied, "No way."

However, I have developed a slight hearing problem, and rather than act like an adult about it, I've decided to ignore it. Sometimes it's annoying to Jerry, and sometimes it even impacts my work.

I was trying a case. The defendants were three young men from the South. I asked them where they were on a particular night around midnight. One of the group decided he was going to be the spokesman, and he said, "Well, about midnight, me and my friends were in the car on our way to Walmart to get some Monsters."

I looked at him as if he was crazy. "You want me to believe that you and your friends got in the car at midnight to go buy *matzohs* at Walmart," I demanded.

There was a stunned silence. Finally, my trusted court officer, Byrd, leaned over to me and said, "No, Judge, not matzohs—Monsters. It's an energy drink." I think that one made it to the blooper reel.

Poor Jerry has to tolerate his otherwise perfect wife having this one slight imperfection. It can get embarrassing.

We lost our beloved dog, Lulu, after fourteen years, and we missed her very much. One day we walked into a local deli and a man waved at me. I didn't know who he was, but sometimes people who are fans of the show wave to me, so I waved back. He got up and approached me.

"Hello, how are you?" he asked, still acting as if he knew me.

"Fine."

"We haven't seen your dog since the spring," he said. We had walked Lulu around the area every day.

"We lost her in May," I said.

"Oh!" He put his hand to his heart. "I'm so sorry."

"But we got two cats," I added.

He looked at me with incredulity, because what he had actually said to me was, "We haven't seen your *daughter* since the spring."

Jerry has since used that embarrassing punch line to punctuate my deafness: "We lost her in May, but we got two cats."

Living together is not easy, with or without marriage. I consider myself a pretty savvy woman, but I have been married three times, twice to the same guy, which suggests that even fairly intelligent people find living with another human being challenging.

Oh, I've heard all those clichés. "He's my best friend!" "We have a fifty-fifty arrangement with mutual respect and excellent communication!" Yadda, yadda, yadda. For me, it has always been that elusive feeling of love that makes all the other crap tolerable.

So by all means try living together. Look for that special feeling. Don't stretch. If it's there, you'll know. It must be mutual. All the other stuff will fall into place, and if it does not, pick yourself up, dust off the bruises, and forge ahead.

I really love living with Jerry Sheindlin, and he ain't easy. Me, I'm a piece of cake.

❖

Made in the USA
Lexington, KY
29 May 2013